PINK T

The Complete Guide On
Everything You Need To Know
About Pink Toe Tarantula

Jackson James

Table of Contents

CHAPTER ONE

INTRODUCTION

A spider's quiet demeanor, minimal space requirements, and relative ease of care can make it a great option for an exotic pet. pink toe tarantulas, sometimes referred to as antilles tree spiders, get their name from their pinkish-orange toes that sprout off of furry black legs. As pets, they require housing that mimics their natural habitat, along with live prey. and keeping in mind that some people do handle their spiders, these animals are more for your enjoyment as you watch their interesting behaviors.

CHAPTER TWO

PINK TOE TARANTULA BEHAVIOR AND TEMPERAMENT

As pets, pink toe tarantulas hush up creatures and will invest a lot of their energy sitting in a relaxing state in their nook. all in all, the most movement you'll see from them is the point at which they're chasing their live prey, for example, crickets, at taking care of time. hope to put in a couple of hours every week on feedings and keeping the nook clean.

These tarantulas can impart a nook to others of similar species, however they don't really require the organization. lone lodging eliminates the danger of human flesh consumption, a circumstance that can happen when the creepy crawlies are living in restricted living arrangements or are generally focused. in like manner, it's ideal to get your tarantula far from some other pets in the family unit, as they could harm each other.

CHAPTER THREE

WHAT YOU NEED TO KNOW ABOUT PINK TOE TARANTULA

While a few proprietors favor not to deal with their arachnids, others appreciate it. also, on the off chance that you do it tranquilly and tenderly, the insect regularly wouldn't fret sitting on your hand or arm. nonetheless, pink toe tarantulas do will in general be restless and might attempt to leap out of your hands on the off chance that they're surprised. this is the reason it's critical to deal with your arachnid while sitting on the ground. in the event that it does unintentionally fall, it will be more averse to get injured. a tumble from even only a couple feet can cause genuine injury or even be deadly to a bug.

Also, a pink toe tarantula may nibble on the off chance that it feels compromised. the insect has poisonous toxin that ordinarily causes a nearby response of redness, growing, and agony like a honey bee sting. be that as it may, a few people who are adversely affected by the toxin can have more genuine responses, for example, trouble breathing, and should look for sure fire clinical consideration.

a walled in area with some stature is essential for these tree-abiding creepy crawlies. a 10-gallon tank with a protected side opening can function admirably. since pink toe tarantulas turn their networks up high, the side opening forestalls harm to the web any time you need to open the nook for feedings or cleaning.

the tank ought to contain 2 to 3 creeps of peat greenery or soil (liberated from manures and pesticides) at the base, just as little logs, branches, and live plants for climbing. examine pet stores for reptile and winged creature frill—

particularly the normal branches—as these frequently function admirably for pet tarantulas to jump on.

CHAPTER FOUR

ANOTHER TEMPERATURE OF PINK TOE TARANTULA

Pink toes can endure a wide temperature range from around 60 to 80 degrees fahrenheit. notwithstanding, in a perfect world the fenced in area temperature should be somewhere in the range of 78 and 82 degrees fahrenheit. under-tank radiators and reptile heat lights can give the right measure of encompassing warmth. screen the temperature with a thermometer in the tank.

in the wild, pink toes live in moist atmospheres, so it's imperative to keep a mugginess level between 65 percent and 75 percent in your bug's walled in area. indeed, keeping the mugginess level high can be one of the most troublesome pieces of having a pink toe tarantula. to raise dampness, you can add a wipe absorbed water to the lower part of the nook, just as fog the fenced in area each a few days with clean water in a shower bottle. not exclusively will this give mugginess to your pet, yet it likewise will profit any live plants in the nook. screen the dampness level with a hygrometer.

to keep the nook clean, eliminate any uneaten prey following 24 hours. additionally, screen for form development, which can happen in a damp climate.

quickly eliminate any segments of the peat greenery or soil bedding that begin to develop shape. also, hope to do a full difference in the bedding generally every four to a half year.

Dropping live prey into the lower part of the walled in area ought to spark your creepy crawly's interest, though the bug may disregard dead bugs. grown-up pink toes for the most part eat a couple of crickets each three to 10 days, and youthful arachnids need comparative sustenance each two to five days. you likewise can give a grown-up tarantula an intermittent pinky mouse or little reptile as a treat. make certain to counsel your veterinarian for the proper sum and assortment to take care of your specific creature. this creepy crawly (likewise called the striped-knee tarantula) is strikingly delightful with a dark body, dark red hairs, white stripes on its legs, and orange spinnerets.

CHAPTER FIVE

CONCLUSION TO PINK TOE TARANTULA

These tunneling 8-legged creature live in enormous networks in the wild and utilize their tunnels to protect their bodies from the brutal temperatures of day and the falling temperatures around evening time. as a pet, the zebra tarantula is very simple to think about; it can adjust to a wide scope of day to day environments. be that as it may, because of its touchy nature, novice bug guardians might need to begin with an alternate animal varieties; this pet requires a middle of the road level of care.

extremely quick, making them a more uncertain possibility for the individuals who like to deal with their pet creepy crawlies. while quiet in air, this creepy crawly shows shooting speeds when surprised; this is a pet that is difficult to catch and hard to contain. attempting to catch and get this sort of tarantula frequently prompts injury of the creature when the creepy crawly falls into its pen or onto the floor from a considerable tallness. nonetheless, with day by day socialization and delicate taking care of, the costa rican zebra tarantula can turn out to be respectably restrained.

A little 5-to-10-gallon aquarium is reasonable for costa rican zebra tarantulas.

the width of the tank should be in any event multiple times more extensive than your bug's leg range; it should likewise be tall enough to oblige a thick substrate for tunneling. the nook should be departure verification. since bugs invest the greater part of their energy climbing, a wire network top is emphatically debilitate. The substrate on the tank's base should be in any event four inches thick and comprise of a blend of peat greenery, soil, or vermiculite. an emptied out log, stopper bark, half of a little mud vase, or a locally acquired insect house can be utilized for a haven. different climbing underpins like phony plants and plants should likewise be arranged all through the fenced in area.

The temperature of your arachnid's environment ought to float around 70 to 85 degrees fahrenheit (21 to 30 degrees celsius) with a moistness level of 75 to 80 percent. supplemental warmth is typically redundant except if you keep your home cool. for this situation, supplement heat by putting an exceptionally planned warming cushion under just one side of your bug's natural surroundings. this permits your pet to move to a cooler area should it need to get away from the glow. vanishing from your bug's water dish should give enough relative stickiness, forestalling the need to fog inside the nook.

FOOD AND WATER

Like most tarantulas, this flesh eater favors eating live prey; it has a solid liking for crickets. this implies that notwithstanding thinking about your pet insect, you will likewise have to painstakingly raise its food source. grasshoppers, scarabs, and cockroaches can likewise be gotten and taken care of to your pet, simply ensure the nourishments you pick have been eating on without pesticide foliage. an intermittent pinky mouse can likewise be offered occasionally for added protein.

Feed your pet tarantula at any rate once every week, taking note of its expansion in hunger. make certain to eliminate uneaten food from the confine, as the development can pressure your creepy crawly; eliminate any rotting stays as they can cause undesirable conditions in the living space.

Give an effectively available water bowl as both a drinking and dampness hotspot for your pet. change the water every day and make certain to gather up any substrate that gets splashed with spills to forestall decay and bacterial development. give spotless and clear non-chlorinated water into a shallow dish. add move out rocks to forestall incidental suffocating in light of the fact that the book lungs (wind stream vents) are situated on the creepy crawly's lower mid-region.

Tarantulas are ordinarily tough types of creepy crawlies that only from time to time become sick. nonetheless, falls are the primary concern to forestall. indeed, even a tumble from a short distance can adequately be to crack a tarantula's eggshell-like midsection, bringing about death. hence, it is important to consistently sit in a low spot (ideally on a covered floor) while dealing with your pet.

Tarantulas can capitulate to lack of hydration, normally because of thoughtless cultivation practice. since tarantulas get the greater part of their hydration from their food, ensure your pet's taking care of timetable is ordinary. changing the water every day and permitting it to dissipate will likewise assist with keeping up hydration levels. be that as it may, on the off chance that you see your arachnid floating over its water bowl and not drinking, it is looking for hydrated air. this is an indication that its current circumstance is excessively dry. you should fog the tank and screen your pet intently.

In the event that your insect will not eat, acts drowsy, and is laying on its back with its legs noticeable all around, don't stress. these are indications of an inevitable shedding—an event that happens every year when a creepy crawly sheds its exoskeleton. disregard your pet during a shed however screen it closely.

When the shedding time frame is finished, eliminate the exoskeleton from the natural surroundings and cease from taking care of your bug or taking care of it for a few days.

THE END

Made in the USA
Monee, IL
20 February 2021

60950324R00022